My First Animal Library

Kangaroos

by Mari Schuh

Bullfrog Books

Ideas for Parents and Teachers

Bullfrog Books let children practice reading informational text at the earliest reading levels. Repetition, familiar words, and photo labels support early readers.

Before Reading

- Discuss the cover photo. What does it tell them?
- Look at the picture glossary together. Read and discuss the words.

Read the Book

- "Walk" through the book and look at the photos. Let the child ask questions. Point out the photo labels.
- Read the book to the child, or have him or her read independently.

After Reading

- Prompt the child to think more. Ask: Can you hop like a kangaroo? Do you carry things in your pockets like a mother kangaroo carries her joey?

Bullfrog Books are published by Jump!
5357 Penn Avenue South
Minneapolis, MN 55419
www.jumplibrary.com

Copyright © 2015 Jump! International copyright reserved in all countries. No part of this book may be reproduced in any form without written permission from the publisher.

Library of Congress Cataloging-in-Publication Data

Schuh, Mari C., 1975– author.
  Kangaroos / by Mari Schuh.
    pages cm. — (My first animal library)
  Audience: Age 5.
  Audience: K to grade 3.
  Includes bibliographical references and index.
  ISBN 978-1-62031-175-2 (hardcover)
  ISBN 978-1-62496-262-2 (ebook)
  1. Kangaroos—Juvenile literature. I. Title.
  QL737.M35S385 2015
  599.2'22—dc23
                                    2014036865

Series Editor: Wendy Dieker
Series Designer: Ellen Huber
Book Designer: Lindaanne Donohoe
Photo Researcher: Jenny Fretland VanVoorst

Photo Credits: All photos by Shutterstock except: Alamy, 8–9, 23br; Corbis, 18–19; Superstock, 14–15; Thinkstock, 10–11, 23tl.

Printed in the United States of America at Corporate Graphics in North Mankato, Minnesota.

For Tom Haythornthwaite—MS

Table of Contents

Fast Hoppers

A kangaroo
hops across
the land.

He hops far and fast.

He lives in a group.

It is called a mob.

The kangaroos graze.

They eat leaves
and grass.

The kangaroo
looks for a mate.

Soon he finds her.

But others find
her, too.

They fight for her.
Kick! Punch! Jab!

He wins!

Now he and the female are mates.

Soon she has one tiny baby.

It is called a joey.

The joey crawls into her pouch.

It drinks her milk for months.

Peek-a-boo!

Wow, the joey has grown!

joey

Let's go!
The joey rides with his mom.

The joey grows up.

It is big and strong.

It hops far
and fast.

Parts of a Kangaroo

ears
A kangaroo's big ears can turn from front to back.

tail
Kangaroos use their long, strong tail for balance when they hop.

front legs
Kangaroos grab leaves and dig holes with their front legs.

pouch
A young kangaroo stays safe and warm in its mother's pouch.

Picture Glossary

graze
To eat
growing grass.

mate
The male or
female partner
of a pair of
animals.

joey
A young
kangaroo.

mob
A group of
kangaroos.

Index

To Learn More

Learning more is as easy as 1, 2, 3.

1) Go to www.factsurfer.com

2) Enter "kangaroos" into the search box.

3) Click the "Surf" button to see a list of websites.

With factsurfer.com, finding more information is just a click away.